W9-CKI-602

Zoom In on
Simple Machines

AP 1 3 '17

Screws

J621.811
RIV

Andrea Rivera

BARRINGTON AREA LIBRARY
505 N. NORTHWEST HWY.
BARRINGTON, ILLINOIS 60010

abdopublishing.com

Published by Abdo Zoom™, PO Box 398166, Minneapolis, Minnesota 55439. Copyright © 2017 by Abdo Consulting Group, Inc. International copyrights reserved in all countries. No part of this book may be reproduced in any form without written permission from the publisher. Abdo Zoom™ is a trademark and logo of Abdo Consulting Group, Inc.

Printed in the United States of America, North Mankato, Minnesota
102016
012017

THIS BOOK CONTAINS RECYCLED MATERIALS

Cover Photo: iStockphoto
Interior Photos: iStockphoto, 1, 4–5, 11, 16, 17, 18, 19, 21; Shutterstock Images, 5, 6–7; Max Oidos/iStockphoto, 8; V. V. Zann/iStockphoto, 9; Kim Schott/iStockphoto, 10–11; Morphart Creation/Shutterstock Images, 13; Andrew Myers/Solent News/Rex Features/AP Images, 14–15

Editor: Brienna Rossiter
Series Designer: Madeline Berger
Art Direction: Dorothy Toth

Publisher's Cataloging-in-Publication Data
Names: Rivera, Andrea, author.
Title: Screws / by Andrea Rivera.
Description: Minneapolis, MN : Abdo Zoom, 2017. | Series: Simple machines |
    Includes bibliographical references and index.
Identifiers: LCCN 2016949161 | ISBN 9781680799552 (lib. bdg.) |
    ISBN 9781624025419 (ebook) | ISBN 9781624025976 (Read-to-me ebook)
Subjects: LCSH: Screws--Juvenile literature.
Classification: DDC 621.8/82--dc23
LC record available at http://lccn.loc.gov/2016949161

Table of Contents

Screws are **simple machines**.
They lift and lower objects.

They also hold objects together.

A screw has
a thread.

The thread is a ridge. It wraps around the screw at an **angle**.

Screws give a **mechanical advantage**.

A **force** is applied to the screw. This makes it turn. The thread drives the screw up or down.

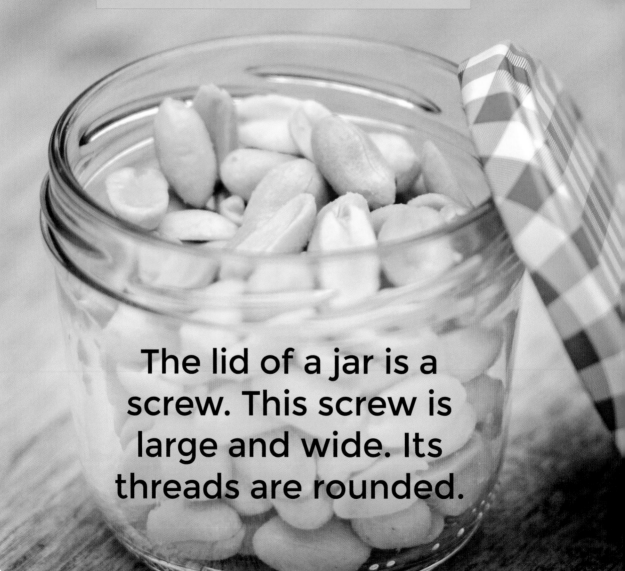

Engineering

The lid of a jar is a screw. This screw is large and wide. Its threads are rounded.

A person turns the lid.
This raises and lowers the screw.
It fastens or unfastens the lid.

The Archimedes screw was used to move water. It lifted the water as it turned.

It helped people
give water to plants
and animals.

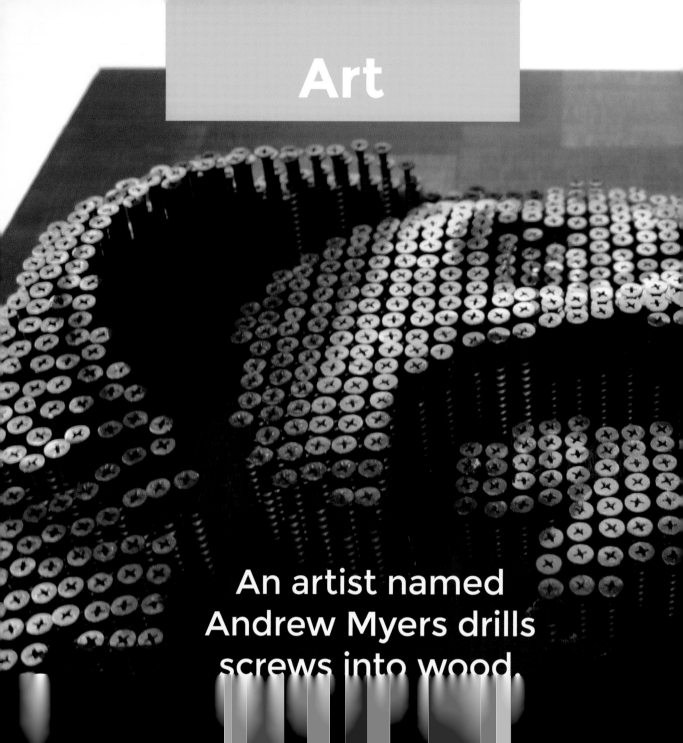

An artist named
Andrew Myers drills
screws into wood.

The screws stick out from the wood. Myers paints the ends of the screws. He makes pictures.

A screw's shape helps
it do its job.

It is shaped like a **cylinder**. Some screws have a point at the end, too.

There are many
kinds of screws.

The tops of some screws are shaped like circles.

Others are hexagons or squares.

- The base of a lightbulb is a screw. It helps a lightbulb fit into a socket. When a person turns a lightbulb, it slides into the socket.

- A carjack can lift part of a car off the ground. It uses a screw. The user turns the screw. This raises the jack.

- A screwdriver is a tool for turning a screw. Turning the screwdriver drives the screw in or out.

Glossary

angle - a slope or a slant.

cylinder - a shape with flat, circular ends and sides shaped like the outside of a tube.

force - a push or pull that causes a change in motion.

mechanical advantage - the way a simple machine makes work easier.

simple machine - a basic device that makes work easier.

Booklinks

For more information
on **screws**, please visit
booklinks.abdopublishing.com

 In on STEAM!

Learn even more with the Abdo Zoom
STEAM database. Check out
abdozoom.com for more information.

Index